Lāna'i

Lāna'i

The Elusive Hawaiian Island—the One that Captain Cook Missed

Anderson Duane Black

VANTAGE PRESS
New York

Maps designed by Denise Hennig

Cover design by Sue Thomas

FIRST EDITION

Published by Vantage Press, Inc.
516 West 34th Street, New York, New York 10001

Manufactured in the United States of America
ISBN: 0-533-13657-1

Library of Congress Catalog Card No.: 00-92078

0 9 8 7 6 5 4 3 2

To those who help Nature elaborate

Contents

One.   A Simple Introduction to a Not-So-Simple Place   1

Two.   Life on Lāna'i Before the Haole (Foreign) Explorers (circa
         1400 A.D. through 1778)   8

Three.   The Haole Arrive on Lāna'i (1779–1901)   12

Four.   The Ranch Years (1901–1922)   18

Five.   Pineapple Reigns as King of the Island (1922–1992)   42

Six.   Resorts—Par Excellence (1992–Present)   71

Seven.   What is the Crystal Ball Forecast for the Future?   77

Further Recommended Reading   79

References   81

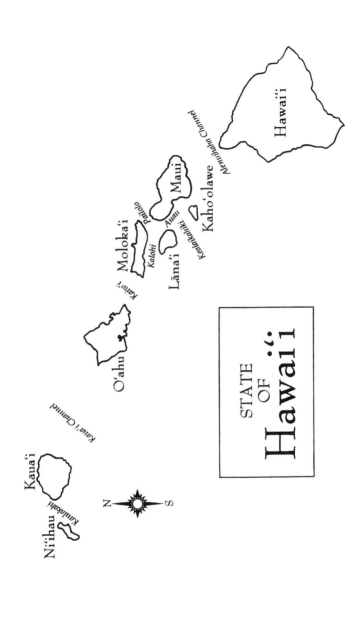

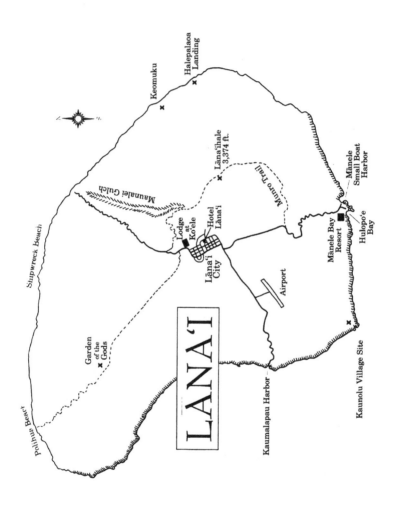

LĀNAʻI

Slipwreck Beach

Polihua Beach

Garden
of the
Gods ✖

Manaʻlei Gulch

Lodge
at
Koʻele

Keomuku ✖

Halepalaoa
Landing ✖

Lānaʻihale
3,374 ft. ✖

Munro Trail

Hotel
Lānaʻi

Lānaʻi
City

Airport

Kaumalapau Harbor

Kaunolu Village Site ✖

Mānele
Small Boat
Harbor

Mānele Bay
Resort

Hulopoʻe
Bay

Lāna'i

ONE
A Simple Introduction to a Not-So-Simple Place

On a bright December afternoon in 1963, I was standing in line at the Hawaiian Airlines check-in counter in Honolulu prior to boarding a vintage DC-3 aircraft destined for the island of Lāna'i. Several years earlier the airline had converted its fleet to larger state-of-the-art equipment; however the company had been compelled to hold back a couple of the DC-3 tail draggers in order to continue servicing their rural station on Lāna'i, due to runway limitations.

A woman standing in front of me—her dress and manner categorized her as a tourist—was endeavoring to buy a ticket to the island and I was intrigued by her conversation with the counter agent.

"Why are you going to Lāna'i?" queried the agent, as she issued the ticket. "Are you sure that's where you want to go? There's nothing there . . ."

This was asked with complete candor and sincerity, and I was interested that an employee of the airline would question a cash-paying customer's destination, so when it was my turn I smiled and asked the agent if she had ever been to Lāna'i.

"No," she answered with a frown. "People don't usually go there unless they're on business—or have family there."

I had moved our family to the island a few months earlier and, reflecting on the comment, realized the agent's beliefs were

1

shared by many residents of the relatively young state of Hawai'i. As a matter of fact, one of my closest friends remarked, after learning I had taken a position on the island with the Dole Pineapple Company, "I've heard the place is so small that when you stand in the middle of the island you can see the ocean on both sides."

These thoughts returned to me as I came across a commentary written in 1914 by William Richards Castle, a lawyer, financier, and second-generation member of a *kama'aina* (long-time) Hawaiian family. In the preface to his book, *Hawaii Past & Present*, which he reported to have written for ". . . a double purpose: to tell those who stay at home something about Hawaii, the youngest of the American Territories; and to help those who are going there to plan their trip intelligently."

His writing, presumably, reflected the knowledge and beliefs of the vast majority of Hawai'i people at that time:

> Two small islands to the south [of the island of Maui] are of little or no interest. Lanai, opposite Lahaina, with an area of 139 square miles, is a single [volcanic] cone 3,400 feet high. On it are springs, one running stream, and some low forest growth, but no cultivation. The Island is given over to cattle and sheep ranches. Kahoolawe, off Makena, covers 69 square miles and is entirely surrounded by low cliffs. It is almost barren, supporting only a few sheep and cattle, and the herdsmen are its only inhabitants. These little islands would not be worth mentioning except that one likes to know their names as the steamer passes between them and Maui on its way to Hawaii.

In 1925, scientist Chester K. Wentworth provided a snapshot of the island's major historical events to that time in the Bishop Museum's publication, *The Geology of Lanai*:

> Lanai was first settled by the Hawaiians about 1400 A.D.—several hundred years after the first Polynesian migrations to Hawaii. The island was first seen by Europeans in 1779, when a part of Captain

Cook's expedition, under the command of Captain Clarke, passed along its south and west coasts. Sailing ships are known to have passed near to Lanai in 1786 and 1787. [George] Vancouver, who explored other islands in the group about 1790, did not land on Lanai. The island is described briefly by the Reverend William Ellis, who saw it in 1823. Several ships are believed to have been wrecked on Lanai during the early part of the nineteenth century.

Active missionary work on the island was begun by ministers from the mission station at Lahaina, Maui, in 1835, at which time the native population was reported to be 1,200. At about this time there was a penal colony for women near the northwest point of Lanai.

In 1855 elders of the Church of Latter-day Saints acquired land from one of the chiefs and settled on the island. Walter Murray Gibson, a leader of the church, arrived in 1861, and in a few years acquired control of much of the best land. After considerable difficulty with the church authorities in Salt Lake City, these lands were inherited at Gibson's death in 1888, by his daughter, Mrs. Talula Lucy Hayselden. A sugar company organized by her husband, Frederick H. Hayselden, and others, failed in 1901. Between 1901 and 1903 the control of Lanai was acquired by Charles Gay and his associates, and in 1910 by Lanai Company. Between 1838 and 1910 the native population decreased from 1,200 to less than 130, partly by removal to other islands.

By 1922 the Lanai Co., which in 1917 came under the exclusive control of Frank F. Baldwin and Henry A. Baldwin, had acquired control of the whole island except the ranch lands of Charles Gay, and about 500 acres remaining under native titles. The entire property of the Lanai Co. [and the lands of Charles Gay soon after] was purchased in December 1922 by the Hawaiian Pineapple Company of Honolulu.

James Drummond Dole's Hawaiian Pineapple Company had acquired the island for the purpose of establishing a substantial pineapple plantation, complementing their farming operations in central Oʻahu. Land was cleared, a town was built, roads were constructed, a water system developed, and a deep water harbor was dredged from which to barge pineapple directly to the company's Honolulu cannery. Lānaʻi City was constructed as a model village—complete with a store, restaurant, a small hospital, a poolroom, a barbershop, a movie house, a church, a bank, and a power plant. Eventually, the operation would come to be known as "The World's Largest Pineapple Plantation."

*   *   *

Question: *Was James Dole the person who, after the overthrow of the Hawaiian monarchy, became the president of the Hawaiian Republic?*

Answer: *No, that was his cousin, Sanford Ballard Dole. Jim had traveled to Hawaiʻi to visit Sanford after recently graduating from Harvard—and stayed on.*

*   *   *

By 1970, Dole Company management had forecasted a likelihood that pineapple production competition from Third World countries would ultimately force Hawaiʻi out of the market, so in an effort to protect their Lānaʻi island real estate investment—as well as the welfare of the some 2,500 residents of the island who were either directly, or indirectly, dependent on pineapple production for their livelihood—established a planning entity called "Lānaʻi Company" (named after the ranch company of days gone by) to plan for the future of the island's lands.

Some twenty years later plantation operations closed, and two world-class resorts opened—supplemented by cattle ranching and diversified agricultural operations—providing an alternative economic base.

This essay traces the social and environmental changes to the island from its volcanic creation to the present, with particular focus on the impact of those peoples who interfaced with the elements of Nature's wilderness, and an assessment of the consequences of those relationships.

A brief geological description is presented for background, followed by notes on Hawaiian spelling style and island place names. And finally, five historical eras are examined: The pre-contact period (circa 1400 A.D.–1779); the discovery period (1779–1901); the ranching period (1901–1922); the plantation period (1922–1982); and the resort period (1982 to present).

The Island's Geology And Climate

In 1940, geologist Harold T. Stearns provided the following description of the island in a hydrology publication of the Territory of Hawai'i:

Lanai lies 59 miles southeast of Honolulu, has an area of 141 square miles, and is 3,370 feet high. . . . The surface above 1,200 feet is generally covered with lateritic [red] soil, which reaches a maximum depth of about 50 feet. Below this level the island is devoid of vegetation and is strewn with boulders, the result of having been once submerged by the ocean to this depth. Traces of various emerged and submerged shore lines are [conspicuous], the highest fossiliferous marine deposits being 1,070 feet above sea level. Lanai is an eroded basaltic volcano built during one period of activity. No secondary eruptions occurred as on most of the other islands. It has three rift zones and a summit caldera. . . .

The climate is semitropical, the mean annual temperature of Lanai City, altitude 1,620 feet, being 68°F. Because Lanai lies to the lee of Maui Island it is dry. The mean annual rainfall ranges from 38 inches on the summit to 10 inches on the coast. . . . Maunalei Gulch has the only perennial stream, and it does not reach the sea.

*   *   *

Question: *Doesn't the word "lanai" refer to something like a porch, or veranda? And also, why is it sometimes spelled with diacritical markings?*

Answer: *The word, lanai, does translate to a porch, or veranda. However, Lāna'i is the name of the island, and translates as "hump"—suggested from the profile of the island as viewed from the island of Maui. See the following spelling notes concerning the 'u'ina (') and macron (⁻).*

*   *   *

Notes on Hawaiian Language Spelling Style

During the past decade in Hawai'i there has been an expanded interest in encouraging linguistic correctness when using the Hawaiian language. An example is the word, "Hawai'i." While the name of the state is still frequently found in print as "Hawaii," most of the state's TV news anchors now utilize the Hawaiian 'u'ina (glottal stop) in everyday newscast operations—thus correctly pronouncing Hawaii, as Hawai-i. Another example is the City and County of Honolulu's recent street name spelling project, wherein the 'u'ina and the macron were incorporated where appropriate.

As a matter of record, the Hawaiian alphabet is comprised of thirteen letters, the vowels a, e, i, o, u, and the eight consonants h, k, l, m, n, p, w, and the 'u'ina, represented by a super-script comma ('). In addition, the Hawaiian "long" vowel is indicated by the use of the macron: ā, ē, ī, ō, and ū.

Anthropologist Kenneth P. Emory, in the introduction to his 1924 classic study of Lāna'i, justifies his reason for *not* using the 'u'ina in the name of the island: "Throughout this paper I have

6

used the glottal stop (') in the spelling of Hawaiian words which possess this stop and which without it are liable to misinterpretation. Lanai, the name of the island, is properly Lāna'i, *but the incorrect spelling* is so fully established that a change seems undesirable [emphasis added]."

This writer has incorporated the 'u'ina and the macron as appropriate, but has left quotations cited in the text as they were published.

Notes on Place Names

Included in Emory's authoritative work (which is recommended for the more-than-just-curious reader) is a combination gazetteer and detailed map of Lāna'i. In his introductory comments to the gazetteer he explains:

With each [place] name is given the geographic feature named and the number locating it on the map, if the location is known.

The translations of the names are classified as applying descriptively if they describe the place named, otherwise they are regarded as commemorative and are classed as formerly descriptive, personal, traditional, or borrowed. Thus, a name describing some object originally at the place or some event commonly happening there, is classified as descriptive. A name of a person who lived at or owned the place is considered as personal. If, however, the name refers to a legendary character, it is classified as traditional or legendary. If the meaning occurs elsewhere and its meaning does not fall within any of the above categories, it is classified as borrowed.

Local place name examples of the above would include: Mānele (sedan chair, or litter); Hulopo'e (name of the man who owned this beach for fishing rights); Lāna'i (hump, profile of the island when viewed from the island of Maui).

TWO

Life on Lāna'i Before the Haole (Foreign) Explorers (circa 1400 A.D. through 1778)

*　　*　　*

Question: *What exactly does the Hawaiian term "haole" mean?*
Answer: *Today, it usually refers to Caucasians, but formerly meant any foreigners.*

*　　*　　*

The late Kenneth P. Emory, one of Hawai'i's most revered archaeologists, conducted an extensive archaeological and ethnographic survey of the entire island of Lāna'i between July 12, 1921 and January 28, 1922, resulting in the classic publication, *The Island of Lanai: A Survey of Native Culture*. In July of 1975, this writer had the privilege of accompanying Dr. Emory, along with a small group of wannabe archaeologists, on a week-long hike around the island wherein he shared his original research notes, and described his experiences.

Dr. Emory reminded us that since there was no written history of the Hawaiian archipelago prior to Captain Cook's advent in 1778, the history of the islands and their inhabitants was recorded by chants and stories handed down from generation to generation. For example, in the chant of Kahakuikamoana it is said that Lāna'i was "found and adopted" by a chief from Tahiti.

Another legend states that long before the time of Wakea and Papa, the Hawaiian islands were pieces of coral caught on the hook of the famous fisherman Kapuheeuanui. At the advice of a priest, the fisherman offered a sacrifice and, after a prayer, called one piece of coral Lāna'i and threw it back into the ocean where it grew into the island of Lāna'i.

According to another legend, the island was inhabited by evil spirits who "killed and ate everybody who came there" until Kaululaau, the son of a Maui Island chief (who lived about 1400 A.D.) killed off the evil spirits and "made it a land fit to be inhabited by human beings." It is believed that about 1425 A.D., during the time of Kakae, Lāna'i first came under Maui rule, and it is thought that during the estimated period of 1550–1660 A.D., the people of the islands of Maui and Lāna'i had a close relationship.

In the 1770s a series of wars were waged between Kalaniopuu, King of Hawai'i, and Kahekili, King of Maui, and in 1776, Kalaniopuu met a humiliating defeat near the sand hills area near Waikapu, Maui. In 1778, Kalaniopuu brought the war to Lāna'i. Kamehameha [The Great] was forty-two years old at the time and accompanied the aged King Kalaniopuu, and Emory reports that in 1922 when he was doing his field work on the island, "The present natives remember the raid as that of Kamehameha." Eventually Kamehameha would establish his "vacation retreat" at Kaunolu on the south side of the island, which would be later visited by his grandson, Lot (Kamehameha V) in 1869, to enjoy the exceptional fishing at the famous refuge of his grandfather.

It was reported that the war on Lāna'i was devastating, with people on every part of the island slaughtered without mercy. In addition, the food supply was destroyed, and much of the island's vegetation was burned off.

Emory summarized the damage in his monograph:

Prior to the raid of Kalaniopuu and his Hawaiian warriors in 1778, Lanai was, in the words of a Maui chief, "a fruitful and populous" island. Captain King passed close to Lanai a few months after the plundering and described it as appearing to be well inhabited, even guessing a population of 20,400. His remarks are surprising in view of the statement written by Menzies [Archibald Menzies, Captain George Vancouver's surgeon] thirteen years later, that "no hamlets or plantations were seen, no trees or bushes adorned the face of the country, which swelled out gradually to a moderate height, so we have reason to think the island is very thinly inhabited."

This much is certain, Lanai was inhabited to such an extent that even the most inhospitable regions show ruins of house platforms, bluff dwellings and garden patches. Since all natural features were taken advantage of as dwelling sites, during periods of maximum population doubtless all the house sites except those under tapu, were occupied.

Legend of The Tomb of Puupehe

Perhaps the most engaging of the traditional Lāna'i island legends for the contemporary visitor is the story of the Tomb of Puupehe—a stone structure erected on the summit of the landmark sea tower that stands approximately 150 feet off the highest point of the cliff separating Mānele Bay (location of the small boat harbor) and Hulopo'e Bay beach, fronting the Mānele Bay Resort.

According to Dr. Emory, who personally investigated the site using rope to scale the 80-foot-high small craggy island, the summit area measures about 70 feet in diameter.

There are several variations to the traditional story. Emory reported that native residents at the time of his investigation (1921–22), said that a girl named Puupehe was "buried here by her lover who took her body from a sea cave where she was drowned [and] with the help of the gods he was able to scale the cliff with the body which he buried beneath the tomb-like structure still conspicuous on the summit of this sea tower." This structure is called Kupapau Puupehe—"Tomb of Puupehe."

Emory's research found earlier versions of the legend to be similar to "the unadorned story [told by modern Lanai natives, with] only deference in the amount of detail . . . [but] with the essentials all present."

Upon investigating the stone platform described in tradition as a burial place, Emory reported ". . . no signs of a burial and some features associated with it indicate use as a religious structure. . . . Observed from the mainland the structure does appear like an enclosure, but on climbing the island I found that the structure is a platform 6 feet wide, 21 feet long and 3 feet high and on it, a little north of center, is a stone 8 inches square and about 18 inches high set in an upright position."

He reported finding no human remains at the sight; however "under the structure and scattered over the top of the island were the bones of many birds, mostly terns, also many egg shells." He surmised that the platform may have been a shrine used by the bird hunters, and concluded that "Puupehe was a bird island and its name, meaning Owl Trap Hill, may be a reflection of its use by bird hunters."

*   *   *

Question: *So how does one find this interesting place?*
Answer: *It's easy for those who enjoy a little exercise. Read on—*

*   *   *

A present day visitor to the island can share in Emory's findings by following the Hulopo'e Bay shoreline to the beautiful sandy cove referred to by locals as Sharks Bay (sometimes Sharks Cove), and then hiking the cliff-side path to its high point. The "Tomb" of Puupehe continues to remain undisturbed 150 feet across from the top of the trail.

11

THREE
The Haole Arrive on Lāna'i (1779–1901)

Although the island of Lāna'i was first made known to the civilized world by the 1779 expedition of Captain James Cook, Cook himself did not see the island, due to his unfortunate demise at Kealakua Bay on the Big Island. Rather, two ships of his fleet, the *Resolution* and the *Discovery* were the first to observe the island. Marguerite K. Ashford, in her classic narrative history, relates that the first actual foreign contact was not made until May 30, 1786, when the *King George* and the *Queen Charlotte*, bound for O'ahu, were met by several canoes off Lāna'i, with "nothing of consequence to barter." In 1787 the *Queen Charlotte*, sailing from the Big Island to O'ahu, again sighted the island and several canoes came alongside to "trade fishing lines for small toes [toys]." In 1791 the American brig *Hope* was met by two double-hulled canoes looking to sell a few "curiosities." Captain George Vancouver sailed past the island in 1792, but did not land.

In later years the Hawaiian Kingdom became more involved with the rest of the world, and ship traffic in the waters surrounding Lāna'i increased; unfortunately however, the island became best known for shipwrecks on its north shore reef, and even today the coastline across the channel from the island of Moloka'i is called "Shipwreck Beach."

Ashford summarizes the period:

Lanai remained quiet and peaceful throughout most of the nine-

12

teenth century. The American missionaries arrived: Lahaina and Honolulu bustled with commercial activity; foreign governments took an interest in the Islands and several diplomatic incidents occurred; the monarchy grew in strength and influence and the transformation of Hawaii began. Throughout all this, life on Lanai remained much the same. Contact with the forces of change at work in Hawaii was minimal, for there was little on Lanai to attract change. The island lacked a natural harbor and there were no stands of sandalwood to lure the chiefs' attention. The missionaries, however, did not neglect Lanai. The people readily accepted the new religion and the accompanying schools, which the missionaries thought essential. A small charcoal industry based on dead *akoko* trees developed later in the century but had little effect on island life.

In 1842 the Protestant converts on the island built two stone churches, and a priest came from Lahaina to hold the island's first Catholic Mass in 1846, but neither considered Lāna'i important, or significant enough to establish resident missionaries. However, in 1850 the first Mormon Elders were assigned to the Kingdom of Hawai'i, comprehended the potential promise of Lāna'i, and in 1854 a group visited the island for the purpose of evaluating the establishment of "a temporal gathering place [a Pacific colony]."

Hawai'i historian Ruth Tabrah relates that later that year:

. . . the Mormons rented a scow from Lahaina which they loaded with cattle, seed, ox yokes, chains and all the supplies necessary to the fledgling colony. They traveled across the channel to Lanai at night to avoid the heat of the daytime. The scow, in the tow of three whale boats rowed by Hawaiians, left Lahaina about nine in the evening and arrived at Kahalepaloa the following morning at eight. Within the next two weeks a thatch house 12x14 was built . . . crops of sweet potatoes, corn, beans and melons were planted . . . and "Iosepa," the City of Joseph, which had been named for their founder, Joseph Smith [had been laid out]. Two main streets were each a mile long running north and south. Two other streets intersected these. By the end of the year, the city had fifteen homes. . . ."

One of the most colorful—and controversial—individuals who came to the island with the Mormons was Walter Murray Gibson, whom the Hawaiians called Kipikona. Gibson and his family would play a significant role in developing ranching and agriculture on the island, and he is credited with acquiring title to much of the native lands—supposedly in the name of the Mormon Church. His later ambitions would entice him to Honolulu where he eventually served under King Kalakaua as Prime Minister, but not before being excommunicated from the Church. Within weeks after his forced separation, several hundred of his native followers deserted the island. Although he was detached from the church, he personally retained title to the Lāna'i lands.

Ashford emphasizes the view that:

Gibson's most important contribution to the history of Lanai was his consolidation of landholding on the island. Gibson worked steadily at acquisition of the Lanai lands from his arrival there until his death. . . . Consolidation by other owners [primarily Charles Gay] in later years was accomplished by building on the base which Gibson made.

However, the impact Gibson had on the island's potential for agriculture was also an important contribution as he continued ranching, and by 1892, the island was referred to as the "principal sheep-growing [lands] in the Kingdom." In addition to goats, hogs, and wild turkeys, Lanai supported 500 horned cattle, 600 horses, and 45,000–50,000 sheep and lambs. Mutton from Lanai supplied the Honolulu and neighbor island markets. Wool in large quantities and of excellent quality was shipped to the United States and Europe.

During the late 1800s a sugar plantation boom occurred in

the Kingdom, and in 1899 one appeared on Lāna'i. Interestingly, the *first* sugar mill in Hawai'i had been established on the island in 1802 when Wong Tze Chun arrived from China on a sandalwood trading ship with a stone mill and a boiler. However, after grinding one small crop he left, taking his grinding stone with him. The 1899 venture was put forth by Gibson's son-in-law, Fred Hayselden, and others on the lower coastal area across from Maui. A wharf was constructed at Halepalaoa, and a railroad bed was laid from the wharf to Keomoku and beyond. (The remains of the abandoned locomotive can still be found with the assistance of a knowledgeable local guide.) The total plantation growing area encompassed some 2,400 acres, and the operation's first crop appeared prosperous. However, late in 1899 the plague struck the area devastating the labor force, and in 1901 the water irrigating the fields turned brackish and the cane's sugar content was nil, forcing the operation to close.

Shipwreck Beach

Shipwreck Beach on Lāna'i is comprised of intermittent stretches of sand, lava rock, and boulders extending along the northern and northeastern shoreline of the island. The most popular stretch for beach combing, however, is the eight-mile section where Lāna'i fronts the island of Moloka'i. With normal trade wind conditions—Hawai'i's most typical weather pattern—this coast is continuously windswept and hammered by the wily currents of the Kalohi and Auau Channels.

The beach itself is guarded by a wide reef which becomes particularly hazardous to ships as the blasting trades charge through the Pailolo Channel separating the islands of Moloka'i and Maui. The two islands create a venturi-like funnel that incites the winds to increase in speed, generating churning seas, propelling flotsam, jetsam, and ill-fated vessels onto the reef—and ultimately onto the beach where they eventually break up over time.

Thus, the name, Shipwreck Beach.

For over one hundred and seventy years the area has been known as a graveyard for sea craft, and in recent times a few have actually been "berthed" there through human design.

The first recorded shipwreck incident on the island was in 1824 when the British vessel *Alderman Wood* foundered on the reef, followed two years later by the American ship *London*, which was carrying a cargo of bullion. Historical records are unclear about how much of the gold and silver was recovered.

*   *   *

Question: *Are you implying that some of the loot may still be around waiting to be found?*

Answer: *Conceivably . . .*

*   *   *

In 1877 the interisland schooner *Iolani* capsized off the coast resulting in two fatalities, and the following year the schooner, *Malolo*, also capsized. Eventually, most of the ships ended up on the beach in bits and pieces.

In more recent years vessels of all shapes and sizes have found a permanent home there. On August 7, 1934, the 34-foot auxiliary yawl *Tradewinds* ended up on the sand when the sharp coral tore a gaping hole in the bottom after going off course en route to Maui from Honolulu, and the schooner *Helene*, out of Port Townsend, Washington, spent a number of years disintegrating on the beach after being caught in the current and driven over the reef.

Long-time locals recall that after World War II several surplus craft were provided residence on the Lāna'i reef as an economical means of disposal. And most broke up to be forgotten.

However, one doggedly remains on the reef and, for present day visitors, has become the predominant highlight of a side-trip to Shipwreck Beach. Interestingly, the ship's name is not known, nor is an exact date of arrival remembered by the old timers. In fact, no one recently questioned could agree on a given year. However, after some debate and recall, most agreed that it showed up after the war—probably in the early 1950s.

*   *   *

Question: *So, why is it still there, riding high on the reef after some forty years?*

Answer: *Because it is made of concrete. According to Honolulu's Hawaii Maritime Center archivist and historian, Stan Melmen, it was presumably one of twenty-two ferrous-concrete oilers built between 1942 and 1944. He reports that there were two basic models: the 366 foot long A1s and the 375 foot A2s. Interestingly, they were never given names, as such. Rather they were assigned numbers, following a prefix, such as YO-144, or YOG-41.*

*   *   *

There were many recorded shipwrecks in Hawaiian waters throughout history, and they are listed in the State Library, the Hamilton Library at the University of Hawaii, and the Hawaii Maritime center. But the concrete ship on Shipwreck Beach will not be found in these lists.

Why?

Burl Burlingame, writer for the *Honolulu Star-Bulletin*, provides a rational answer: "Technically, since the ship was beached, it's not a shipwreck." Wryly, he concludes: "But Beached Beach doesn't have the same cachet as Shipwreck Beach."

FOUR
The Ranch Years (1901–1922)

Charles Gay of Kauai began investing in the island of Lāna'i in 1902 and by 1907 owned all of Lāna'i with the exception of about 100 acres of kuleana [small pieces of private property] land. Gay acquired title in fee simple to the lands, and since that time the single ownership facet of the island has been preserved; all subsequent transactions involving large parcels of land on Lāna'i have entailed the transfer of essentially the entire island. However, the acquisitions had left Gay financially strapped.

But the Gay family had fallen in love with Lāna'i. They built a private school at Ko'ele to educate their own children plus those of the ranch hands, and hired a Hawaiian woman with a master's degree in education to operate the school. (The public school at Keomuku village was fifteen dusty miles away down on the beach across the channel from Lahaina.) Charles Gay kept a church at Keomuku open to Christians of all faiths, and encouraged the Catholic priest from Maui to come frequently to hold mass for the Catholics of Lāna'i.

Their comfortable and roomy mountain home, *Lalakoa*, was located at 1,800 feet above sea level, and a mile east of the ranch headquarters at Ko'ele. (The ranch site is now the location of the Lodge at Ko'ele resort, and the Lalakoa homestead, later to become a Dole pineapple field, is now the site of The Experience at Ko'ele championship golf course.) Unfortunately, after three years of a drought ending in 1909, the Gays would lose their lands—except for six hundred acres in the Lalakoa area—to a *hui* [investment group] for $375,000, and the *hui* then formed Lānaʻi Company.

George Munro was brought from New Zealand to manage the new Lānaʻi Company and instructed by the owners to shift the island's emphasis from sheep to cattle, including fencing off the watershed forest lands. It should be noted that Gay had already taken steps toward protecting the watershed and controlling the environmentally destructive goat population.

Zschokke, in a 1930 tree planting manual contended that: ". . . the feral goat is presently the most destructive creature in the Hawaiian ecosystem (excluding, of course, man); [uncontrolled] cattle and sheep were possible contenders for this destruction in the past. . . ."

In 1911 a head count recorded 179 cattle and 20,588 sheep; by 1917, Munro reported 4,000 cattle were grazing on the lands but only 2,600 sheep.

Under Munro's environmentally focused stewardship, strenuous efforts were put forth to reforest the island's single volcanic mountain (Lānaʻi Hale) with Norfolk Island pines after their ability to attract moisture from clouds passing through their needle covered boughs was discovered. Today, Lānaʻi is known for its Norfolk and Cook Island pine forests marching along every ridge and piercing the clouds passing over Mt. Lānaʻi Hale.

[Author's note: During the early 1970s, Lānaʻi had become a leading commercial producer of Norfolk Island pine seeds, and one international seed marketer told this writer that there were "more Norfolk Island pines on Lānaʻi than on Norfolk Island—located off the eastern coast of Australia."]

In 1918 the Libby food company had taken an option to buy the island for the purpose of expanding their pineapple operations, but later decided against going ahead with the acquisition. Instead, two brothers from Maui, Frank and Harry Baldwin, acquired Lāna'i for a cattle ranch and game preserve for $588,000, and in 1920 introduced Axis deer from the island of Moloka'i.

*　　*　　*

Question: *Hold on now! Are the trees Norfolk Island Pine, or Cook Island Pine?*
Answer: *A lot of old-timers have been confused for the past several years. Read on—*

*　　*　　*

Long-time residents of Lāna'i City have always been conspicuously aware of living among towering forests of Norfolk Island pine trees, and—legend has it, as noted above—that the island's watershed on Mount Lāna'i Hale was planted to the Norfolks under the direction of ranch manager George Munro during the later half of the ranching era, and the early years of the plantation. However, soon after the first resort opened, books and pamphlets were describing the trees as being Norfolk Island *and* Cook Island pines—for example, see Savrann's *Lana'i Hawaii*. This writer was intrigued, as some twenty-five years earlier a visiting architect-planner from Honolulu had sat sipping coffee on the veranda of the Lāna'i Inn (now Hotel Lāna'i), glanced out over the community and announced: "It appears that there are two different kinds of pines growing here."

It now seems that *he* was in error, as *all* of the trees he was viewing have since been identified as Cook Island pines, even though astute observers can usually identify minor variations among individual trees. However, the academically curious (led by third generation Lāna'ian Gary Onuma who directs Lāna'i Company's game management activities), have attempted to catalogue such variations in an effort to separate out and identify the *real* Norfolks; and such study has led back through the years to Walter Murray Gibson and his son-in-law Fred Hayselden, key players of the foreign discovery era—and Charles Gay and George Munro of the ranch period. Tracing the introduction of the Norfolk is a fascinating tale, commencing with a tuberculosis-ridden Dr. Willhelm Hillebrand moving from Prussia in 1857 to the Sandwich Islands in search of a healthier place to live.

Hillebrand, a medical doctor, not only regained his health, but served his adopted country well. A favorite of the royal family (who he included as his patients), he served as a member of the Board of Health, and was a member of the Privy Council in the court of Kamehameha V. In April 1865, as commissioner of the bureau of immigration, he traveled to China, India and Malaya to arrange for the importation of laborers, and later in 1878, he arranged for the emigration of 180 Portuguese from Madeira and the Azores.

Long associated with the Royal Hawaiian Agricultural Society, he also arranged for the importation of a myriad of seeds, and useful and ornamental plants desirable for growing in the bleak and dusty Honolulu of that day. He was also personally responsible for planting many of the trees, now veritable giants, standing about the grounds of The Queen's Hospital, and especially those on the spacious grounds of his former Honolulu homestead located on the corner of Vineyard and Nuuanu Streets—known today as Foster Botanical Gardens.

Among his close associates was young John Lydgate who chronicled several of Hillebrand's efforts to gather and study botanical specimens around the Hawaiian Islands. What follows are excerpts from Lydgate's "Reminiscences Of An Amateur Collector," of their trip to Lāna'i to visit Walter Murray Gibson in 1870:

The only way to get to Lanai in those days was to make the trip in an open boat [from Lahaina] with a Hawaiian crew. We made it in three or four hours before fresh trades with the wind on our beam, the spray coming over the sheets and the cranky boat lifting and

21

careening far over, until you held your breath and thought she was never coming back again. . . .

As we neared Lanai, we ran into smoother water, and early in the afternoon landed at the little native hamlet of Ka-hale-palaoa. As I remember it, there were half a dozen grass houses there, with the traditional easy-going population of men, women, children and dogs, and none of them doing anything. To our insistent demand for horses, just as soon as possible, to carry us over to Palawai, a dozen or so miles away, we got an indifferent reply, that the horses were all out on the kula [open land] and couldn't be got in a hurry.

. . . we finally secured two passable saddle horses and a pack horse, and set off over the mountain trail that crossed the ridge to the other side of the island, where was located the Gibson ranch of Palawai. . . .

We arrived . . . just before dark and were very glad of the cordial reception we got at the hands of the distinguished looking Walter Murray. There was certainly nothing impressive in the surroundings. A main grass house in which the family lived, I should say, about 20 by 30, another which served as kitchen and dining room, a third of that size, with a Chinese cook in command, and a third cottage of the same kind, somewhat farther, for guests, which was assigned to us.

For dinner we had roast mutton—very excellent in quality—boiled rice with molasses, and coffee.

Lydgate went on to describe the following days wherein he and Hillebrand searched and explored the island, collecting botanical specimens, sometimes with Gibson as their leader:

At the very summit of the island, which is generally shrouded in mist, we came upon what Gibson called his lake—a little shallow pond, about the size of a dining table. In the driest of times there was always water here, and one of the regular summer duties of the Chinese cook was to take a pack mule and a couple of kegs and go up to the lake for water. . . .

22

Our stay was cut short somewhat prematurely, after we had been there some two weeks. One afternoon, as we were fighting our way down a wooded slope, through a stubborn scrub jungle, we heard voices calling to us from below, "E ka haole kauka, auhea oe?" ("You, foreign doctor, where are you?") We responded and hastened down as fast as we could and found the boat's crew from Lahaina, with a note from the American consul there begging Dr. Hillebrand to make all possible haste over, as his wife was grievously ill and they feared for her life.

There was nothing for it but to hasten home, pack up our traps and our valuable plant collections, say farewell to the Gibsons and set out for Lahaina with the returning boat. We did this, but with reluctance. We found, on arriving at Lahaina that the invalid lady was a good deal of a hypochondriac, and that a few days, or even a week later would have done just as well. But there was no going back to Lanai, and anyway, there was plenty of exploring to be done on Maui.

That was the only visit of Hillebrand to the island, but a future event would make a lasting impact—the introduction of the Norfolk Island pine. According to George Munro in an unpublished memoir written around 1955:

When I visited Lanai in 1902, there was a small grove of eucalyptus trees of several species and a tall Norfolk Island pine by the manager's house. [This is the same tree that stands in front of the Lodge at Koele today.] If my memory serves me rightly, Dr. Garrit Wilder told me that Dr. Hillebrand introduced six of these pines, probably from Australia. Two were sent to Mr. Meyer on Molokai, two to Maui (probably to Captain McGee of Ulupalakua) and two to Lanai [presumably to Gibson, or his son-in-law Fred Hayselden, who at one time lived in the manager's house]. One of them died but the other is still living. A few years ago, I was told that it was measured by a surveyor and found to be 134 ½ feet high.

Munro continues:

When we took up our residence in the old Hayselden home at Koele, the Norfolk Island pine tree which they planted in 1875 was between 75 and 100 feet high and overhung the house. We were impressed when the breeze was blowing during the foggy weather by the noise of the water collected on its foliage falling on the iron roof of the dining room and veranda below.

He went on to describe the planting of Norfolks for the benefit of the fog drip (to catch the moisture in the fog), and how they decided to plant the trees on the mountain for the benefit of the island's underground water system.

Over a period of several years, several hundreds of trees were planted. Seed was difficult to obtain as few of the old trees in Hawaii at that time had seeded. However, I got some and made the first planting in the forest with seedlings about a foot high.

The last time I was in the Lanai forest was in 1955 when I had the pleasure of driving over the mountain on the Hawaiian Pineapple Company's new automobile road and which they had generously named the Munro Trail.

*   *   *

Question: *So, where did the Cook Island pines come from?*
Answer: *Read on—*

*   *   *

Hawaii state forester Robert Hobdy grew up on the island and contends that the huge Norfolk at Koʻele is the *only* one on the island, and the rest are all Cooks. This seems to be visually corroborated, as the lone tree at Koʻele has an obviously distinct profile compared to all of the other pine trees on the island. One could argue that this might be due to the difference in the ages of the trees, but photographs of the Koʻele tree taken in the early part of this century show it with essentially the same basic characteristics as observed today.

"They are closely related," according to Hobdy. "They have the same genus, *Araucaria*, but the Norfolk is the species *Heterophylla*, while the Cook is *Columnaris*."

So, again, where did the Cook pines come from? And why have they been referred to as Norfolks throughout the years?

As the trees were obviously not propagated from the Norfolk seedling introduced by Hillebrand in 1875, it can be assumed that seeds were introduced by others, probably from Australia or New Zealand. That suggests several possibilities, since Gibson's son-in-law, Fred Hayselden, was originally from Australia, and Gay was from New Zealand, as was George Munro (who later reported asking his brother in New Zealand to send him various other seeds for propagation)—so, they are all manifest suspects. Also interesting is that each family, in their time, lived in the ranch house adjacent to the great pine. However, Munro's unpublished work clearly indicates that he was collecting Norfolk [apparently, Cook] seeds from trees already established on the island, so that leaves Hayselden or Gay. Hayselden's major focus was managing the Gibson lands, especially sheep ranching and establishing a sugar plantation along the Keomuku coast opposite Maui, so that would seem to suggest Charles Gay, who in hindsight might be classified as a "social-environmentalist" [author's term]. Readers can draw their own conclusions, or develop hypotheses that fit their views of the evidence.

*   *   *

Question: *Okay. So why were the trees referred to as Norfolk Island pines down through the years?*

Answer: *"Because," explains Hobdy, "professional foresters referred to them as Norfolk until the middle of this century."*

Shipwreck Beach—a lonely beachcomber's paradise. Photo by John Schaumburg.

The sea tower, Puupehe, is the site of a famous legend. Photo by Anderson Duane Black.

The "Tomb of Puupehe" is still conspicuous at the summit of the sea tower. Photo by Anderson Duane Black.

Monument near Halepaloa landing commemorates workers who died during the 1898 plague. Photo by Anderson Duane Black.

Ruins of Protestant church built in 1852 near present day Lāna'i City. Photo by Anderson Duane Black.

Before pineapple, much of the upper island lands were covered by cactus. (Photo courtesy of Dole Archives, circa 1918)

In 1926, James Dole invited business and government leaders to tour his Lānaʻi venture. Model T Fords imported for the day would stay behind for use by plantation foremen. (Photo courtesy of Dole Archives)

Honolulu visitors tour the recently completed Buddhist Church. Shortly after December 1941, the resident minister would be seized for internment, and the church closed. (Photo courtesy of Dole Archives, circa 1923)

Public school classroom located near Koʻele Ranch. (Photo courtesy of Dole Archives, circa 1926)

Plantation manager Harold Bloomfield-Brown and his Model T Ford—sans chauffeur. (Photo courtesy of Dole Archives, circa 1923)

Field workers harvesting pineapple. Photo by Werner Stoy, circa 1960.

Shipwreck off of Shipwreck Beach. The World War II oiler has rested on the reef for half a century. Photo by John Schaumburg.

Nature perfected: Gardens at the Lodge at Ko'ele. Photo by Anderson Duane Black.

Clubhouse at the Experience at Koʻele golf course. Photo by Anderson Duane Black.

The majestic Norfolk Island Pine planted in 1875 towers above the Lodge at Koʻele today. Photo by Anderson Duane Black.

Looking across Hulopoʻe Beach to the Manele Bay Hotel. Photo by Anderson Duane Black.

FIVE

Pineapple Reigns as King of the Island (1922–1992)

Plantation life in the Hawaiian Islands was a remarkable combination of ethnic and socio-economic lifestyles, but the plantation experience on the Island of Lāna'i was singularly unique when compared to other Hawaiian island locations.

The first phrase of the above statement mirrors the social history of the past one hundred and fifty years in Hawai'i (give or take a decade), where people congregated from around the world, and over time created a truly special blended society. However, the plantation experience was frequently more intense, particularly where a plantation was isolated from urban communities. For example, life on a sugar plantation situated in the isolated North Kohala District of the Big Island was quite different from that of a plantation set on the outskirts of the flourishing seaport town of Hilo on the same island.

There are several reasons why the Lāna'i experience was uncommonly unique compared to other plantations. For one thing it was a Johnny-come-lately operation, not founded until 1922. In contrast, the sugar trade originated during the monarchy, while the pineapple industry didn't get underway until the turn of the century when recent Harvard grad James Drummond Dole sailed into Honolulu Harbor and kick-started the farming and packaging technology required to develop offshore markets for the "King of Fruit."

Another thing that made the Lāna'i experience different was that other plantations in Hawai'i were established on islands with developed centers of commerce, i.e., Honolulu, on the island of O'ahu; Hilo and other communities on the Big Island; Wailuku and Lahaina on Maui; and Lihue on Kaua'i. Lāna'i as an island, however, was without a commercial center. It was an isolated island ranching community whose modest population lived off the land and sea—and cruised the nine-mile Auau channel to Lahaina several times a month to acquire their additional necessities.

During the early 1990s, one social observer pondering the island's economic shift from what had been once lauded as the World's Largest Pineapple Plantation to a world-class tropical resort, referred to Lāna'i as ". . . an island in transition."

In retrospect, however, the Lāna'i island community has been in transition—that is, experiencing substantial social change—since pineapple came on the scene in 1922. At that time the new plantation complemented the existing cattle ranch, which continued to operate until 1954. Before the arrival of the plantationers, the island's population was somewhere around 115 people, mostly of Hawaiian lineage, but with the establishment of pineapple the number soon expanded to 750. Within a few years the population grew to several thousand, and a majority of those new people were of Asian descent.

The concept of "transition" is perhaps most easily appreciated by old-timers who have occupied a locale for an extended period: "Back in the old days things were different. . . ." Usually, change in a community is recognized over periods of time, perhaps covering a decade . . . possibly two or three decades . . . maybe more.

For example, in the case of Lāna'i, the planning for an alternative economic base officially commenced in the fall of 1970 when Lāna'i Company was established by its parent organization, Castle & Cooke, Inc. (later called Dole Food Company) to "plan for the future use of the Lāna'i island lands" two decades prior to the opening of the Lodge at Koele and the Manele Bay resorts.

*   *   *

Question: *What was day-to-day life like on a remote pineapple plantation in those early days?*

Answer: *To best recount life during the plantation years, we have included four oral history snapshot views of families who settled on the island during different phases of the plantation period's seventy years. Brief background notes, and/or plantation bulletins or news clippings, are provided to set the stage for each interview.*

*   *   *

The Nobu Kuwada Family

In the spring of 1967, Nobu Kuwada retired, ending 41 years of service with the plantation's engineering department. He was interviewed by this writer for a feature article in the plantation's monthly newsletter, and the following oral history transcription—with the addition of [bracketed] explanatory notes—is a product of that interview:

Nobu Kuwada: I crossed the channel from Maui to Lāna'i in the early spring of 1926 when I was employed as a floor hand machinist at Pioneer Mill [a sugar plantation in Lahaina] and assigned to the locomotive and stationary steam engine repair. Jim Munro, an engineer at Lāna'i Plantation, was having mechanical problems with a road roller and I was ordered to offer assistance. When the work was finished Mr. Munro offered me a job with Dole, or Hawaiian Pine as it was called in those days. Since the company on Lāna'i was a young and growing organization, I decided advancement opportunities should be good and I accepted a job as a general mechanic.

I returned to Lahaina and stayed for about a month while a new man was found to take my place at Pioneer. Our only child at that time, Hatsue, was just two years old, and we decided I should move to Lāna'i by myself in order to get our new home ready. My wife Shizue and Hatsue followed about two weeks later.

We lived in a small house which stood where the Union Hall [near the center of town] is now located. The community was grouped along ethnic lines and we lived in a block with about ten other Japanese families. A community toilet, as well as a community bath-house, was shared by everyone living in the block.

As I recall, the stores were quite similar to those we have today [1967] except that fewer items were stocked on the shelves. Lāna'i-grown beef and pork, as well as locally-caught fish were sold over the counters. Vegetables, chicken and eggs came from off-island.

The Okamoto Store was located in the building now housing Richard's Shopping Center, and the Yet Lung Store occupied the building where Genevieve Oshiro currently operates the Fun House [now, Maui Community College's Lāna'i Learning Center]. The Shiozawa Bakery was in the Pine Isle Market building and the theater and bank were already in their present locations. The hospital had been built and old Dr. Wilkinson served as the plantation physician [not to be confused with Dr. "Bill" Wilkinson who practiced on the plantation between 1941 and 1952].

A structure housing the Hawaiian Pine office and the U.S. Post Office was located on what is now the front lawn of the present Dole Administration Building. Later that building was moved across the street, where it stands today, to be used for post office business exclusively [which explains why the Post Office flagpole stands across the street from the Post Office]. Only the main streets were paved.

The weather seemed awfully cold in those days; in fact, we used to go out in overcoats. I suppose coming from warm, balmy Lahaina made us feel cold and you must consider the fact that there were no trees to break the winds coming off Lāna'i Hale. [Photographs taken in 1926 show the pine trees to be about three feet high.]

Lāna'i City had a reputation for being the cleanest town in the Territory of Hawaii. The plantation had yard workers assigned to various sections of the town and each morning yards were raked of leaves and rubbish.

The school was up at Ko'ele near the present location of the No. 1 green on the [Cavendish] golf course and, as I remember, consisted of one building. Mrs. James Munro was the principal.

However, not everyone lived in Lāna'i City proper. In addition to those at Ko'ele Ranch, there were camps located at both Miki and Palawai [south of Lāna'i city in the direction of the present airport]. As I recall, 50 to 60 families lived at Miki camp and 5 or 6 lived at Palawai. Mule stables were also located at each camp in addition to three in Lāna'i City.

A one-ton Ford truck furnished daily transportation to and from Lāna'i City and the school for families living in the outlying camps. Transportation to and from the island was by water only. The S.S. *Miki Ala* was operated by the Inter-Island Steamship Navigation Company and stopped at Lāna'i on its trips between Honolulu and Hilo.

The trail to Manele [now the site of the Manele Bay Resort] was not even passable by wagon in 1926 and we would walk 2 to 3 hours just to go fishing. However, you could get down to Keomuku [across the channel from Maui] with a wagon and team.

The first water developed at Maunalei [a deep gulch on the windward side of the island, facing the islands of Maui and Moloka'i] was developed back in the ranching days before the island was bought by Hawaiian Pine. However, the volume of water was inadequate for the plantation's operations for many years and irrigation was impossible. In addition, the lack of water made the installation of indoor plumbing systems impractical. During dry periods, we had to be very careful of how we used what water we could get.

The first airport was established in an open field on the edge of town [near the riding stables at the Lodge at Ko'ele], and the old biplanes landing on the grass were a source of real excitement for the children.

The [first] manager of the plantation was Harold Bloomfield-Brown and he managed with a strong hand. Through the years, Brown has become a legend and not necessarily a popular one. To many, both on and off the island, he was the "governor" of Lāna'i. To visit the island, you had to have a permit signed by Brown. Those who lived on Lāna'i had to have a permit to buy a car, and these were not easy to obtain.

Motorcycles were not allowed, nor were chickens or gardens in your backyard. The manager's major reason for not wanting many private vehicles on the island was to reduce the possibility of having accidents. To further this goal, the children were not allowed to play on the roads. Mr. Brown was always immaculate and well-dressed and wanted the community to appear the same.

Jim Dole, the company's founder, was an ambitious and energetic man who had a great feeling for the soil and particularly for pineapple. In January of 1926, a congregation of businessmen and government officials, including congressmen, legislators, and the governor of the territory, Wallace Ryder Farrington, accompanied Mr. Dole on a tour of Lāna'i. When the group got up to an untilled area, Dole picked up a handful of dirt, sniffed it, and said, "Pineapple will grow well here."

Model T Fords were used by the foremen, and job foremen [first line supervisors] carried out their duties on horseback. Between 1929 and 1932, we had increased the number of White trucks to 40 and all of the old solid tire models had been converted to pneumatic tires.

When the Depression hit, the pineapple market took a drop. Pineapple was still considered a luxury item in those days and few housewives could afford to buy more than the necessities. Pineapple production was cut back to what the market could handle and Dole stock at one time was down to $1 a share.

Many people left Lāna'i during the Depression and some returned later on. Many of those who stayed were only offered 2–3 days of work a week and "make-work" projects were alternated among the different work gangs on the island by government work project programs.

However, things started to pick up in 1933–34 and by 1936 the plantation was almost back to normal. In fact, by the end of 1936 almost all of the homes and buildings making up Lāna'i City today had been built. Miki and Palawai camps had been phased out and those families now lived in Lāna'i City. The pineapple market had recovered, and labor was abundant. Times were starting to be good, and a better and easier way of life on Lānai was occurring as "modern conveniences" were introduced into the island's homes.

The domestic water system was developed in 1939 at Maunalei and by 1941, lean-tos had been added to most of the homes in the city to house the newly installed bathrooms, and one by one the community bath- and wash-houses were phased out.

December 7, 1941, brought a different kind of change to Lāna'i. Following the attack on Pearl Harbor, over a hundred members of the military were stationed on the island—some patrolled the shorelines, while others were stationed in the hills.

Most of the soldiers were from New York State. They were nice boys and I don't recall the community having any trouble with the military people. The Army was headquartered in an area just inside the eastern edge of town.

Like most of Hawai'i we were blacked-out during the war and before the military arrived, civilian patrol groups walked the streets of the community checking houses for blackout violations.

Fishing was by military permit only, and only United States citizens were allowed to fish. This resulted in really good fishing for those of us who could get permits, since the absence of fishermen allowed the fish populations to build up.

Pineapple sales were high and business prospered as the government was buying a lot of fruit, and all through the period the company developed more land for pineapple cultivation.

As the war ended, many of our men, especially the skilled workers, were lured away to Honolulu and elsewhere by the Territory's expanding economy, and we were faced with an increasingly growing labor shortage. The Norfolk Island pines were now twenty-two years old and not only served as effective windbreaks, but had given the community a pleasingly "different" appearance. Our family had grown too, and now we had added Richard, Nobue, Yoshie, and Toshie to our clan.

Trucks and tractors had replaced the mules as a chief source of power and locomotion on the plantation, and more automobiles were seen on the streets in town. As I look back now, I realize that the growing of pineapple was starting to become an art while the pineapple industry as a whole was becoming a science.

At the end of the War many of the Chinese, Koreans, and Puerto Rican workers moved away to engage in the activities that were developing with the Territory's post-war expansion and development. To meet the growing shortage of labor left by this migration we turned to the Philippine Islands and in 1966 many of those who came in 1946 received their 20-year service awards.

The period from the early '40s to the mid–'50s marked the beginning of many new ways of life on Lāna'i. The idea of living in racial group clusters gave way to an integrated community where everyone was mixed together. During the mid–'40s the ILWU [union] organized many of the plantation employees throughout Hawaii which had many far-reaching effects on both business and society.

Transportation was rapidly changing. Inter-island steamship

service had ended in 1941, and during 1946 the airport was moved from the edge of the community to its present location four miles south of the town. At first the new airfield consisted of a dirt runway which was sprayed with sea water each night during dry weather to keep the dust down. Later oil was used as a dust treatment and in 1951 the runway was paved.

In 1954 the ranch was phased out and most of the cowboys transferred to the plantation operation.

Perhaps the most important event that occurred during that period was when employees were offered the opportunity to purchase their homes—along with the land. The result of this has been that today approximately sixty percent of the homes in Lāna'i City are owned in fee simple by their occupants.

As I look back on my 40 years on Lāna'i, I now realize that I and my fellow workers who came here during those early days were pioneers. We came to a virgin land and helped build it into the world's largest plantation.

Author's note: Nobu Kuwada died in November, 1969.

The Nunotani Family

Article printed in *The Lanaian*, October 6, 1950:

Brief History of Buddhism on Lanai

by

Harry Nunotani

It was a quarter century ago when the Hawaiian Pineapple Company saw the need of a church for the Buddhist people on Lanai, and undertook the work of building a suitable structure, which was completed in July, 1925. Mr Bloomfield-Brown, Mr. Sanzo Tanigawa and Mr. Ruth were some of the few who were very instrumental in bringing this about.

The new church was dedicated with an appropriate ceremony on December 13, 1925, with the late Bishop Imamura officiating and assisted by Reverend Yoshio Hino, the first minister to be installed here. . . .

The Reverend Kiyohira became the minister in 1941 and served only four months, when on that fateful day in December 1941, he was seized for internment.

Then for four ensuing years the Buddhist people on Lanai were without the services of an ordained priest. The church was closed, the image and all of the altar ornaments were carefully boxed and stored at the Cemetery by the late Mr. Kosuke Okamoto. It was only through his painstaking care in wrapping these individual articles that even after four years of storage they were found to be in perfect condition. Mr. Jusaku Minami substituted as a priest and read services at funerals and memorials during the war years.

Then in January, 1946, when Reverend Tadao Kouchi returned from the Mainland, plans were formulated to seek the reopening of the church.

Through the kind efforts of Mr. Dexter Fraser, manager of the Hawaiian Pineapple Company, the present building, which was formerly used as a restaurant, was remodeled and turned over to the Buddhist people. The building was completed and opened for worship on April 20, 1946.

Author's note: Harry Nunotani started his career with the Hawaiian Pineapple Company in 1928 as an 18-year-old laborer, and was eventually assigned to the personnel office. His years in personnel ended in 1946 when he was transferred to the Dole Community Trust, which later became Plantation Housing, Ltd.

He served as Housing Administrator with Plantation Housing until it was phased out in 1965, and at that time was transferred back to the personnel department, taking the housing function with him. In the early 1970s, when housing was transferred to the newly formed Lāna'i Company, Harry continued to oversee the company's housing unit.

Story from *Lanai In Focus*, March 15, 1975:

Nunotani Retires after 47 years

Harry Nunotani, Lanai Company Housing Supervisor, will retire on April 1, after 47 years of service with Castle & Cooke on Lanai.

Mr. Nunotani was born in Kohala on the Big Island, and attended Kohala High School. He moved to Lanai and joined the company in 1928, and spent nearly all of his career in housing.

He was affiliated with the housing function on the island for so long, in fact, that he is probably one of the best known persons on the island. There are few Lanaians who have not had some association with him through the years.

Harry and his wife, Kimiyo, plan to "do a little of this and a little of that" and enjoy their well-earned retirement.

Author's note: The following interview took place in the home of Harry and Kimiyo Nunotani on March, 28, 1995.

Harry: I was born in March of 1910, in the sugar plantation town of Hawi in the North Kohala District of the Big Island. I was eighteen when I graduated from Kohala High School and came to Lāna'i on the interisland steamer *Claudine* in 1928 with my younger brother, James, who was sixteen at the time. Lāna'i was like a "new country" with fresh opportunities.

Kimiyo: I was born in Wahiawa, and when I was six years old I went to Japan, graduated from school there, and when I was fourteen I returned to Hawai'i . . . to Lāna'i . . . where my father had been since 1923. He had his own fields [a small farm] in Wahiawa [on the island of Oʻahu], but because my mother died he sold that land and came here.

On the island of Lānaʻi he worked directly for Mr. Brown [Harold Bloomfield-Brown, the island's first plantation manager] as a right-hand-man, and chauffeured him around in his automobile.

Harry [laughing]: It was a Model T Ford.

Where did you live, Kimiyo?

Where did I live?

When your father was driving Mr Brown around . . .

My father had a house by what is now called Lānaʻi Avenue. Third house down from the old fire station that was located on the corner of Lānaʻi Avenue and Ninth Street.

Now . . . how did you meet this guy? [Harry chuckles]

His mother used to come my house every day because I got education in Japan.

So, how did you get married? [Kimiyo places the palms of her hands together, and Harry chuckles.] *Your parents arranged for you to get married?*

Yes.

What year was that?

We've been married sixty-one—March 2, 1934—sixty-one years.

You say that your father worked for Harold Bloomfield-Brown. Did you like him?

Oh yes. He was a wonderful man. When I came back from Japan—every Tuesday he would come to pick me up and take me up to his home. I couldn't understand English, but somehow he could understand what I said. He had a "big shots" room where he entertained important visitors.

How old were you then?

I was fourteen, fifteen . . .

How old were you when you got married?

Nineteen.

53

And, how old was Harry?

Twenty-four. [Harry chuckles in the background]

Harry, did you have any contact with Brown?

Well, yeah, no. Not really . . .

Kimiyo: When we got married—he was so happy.

Mr. Brown was happy when you got married?

He gave us the house next to the fire station to live in [on what is now the corner of Ninth and Lāna'i Avenue].

You moved into the house next to the old fire station?

We lived there until 1943 . . . then we moved here. [A comfortable plantation-style home on Ilima Street]. This block was only for the *Luna* [plantation supervisors].

Tell me about having children back then.

Kimiyo: Shirley was born in 1935.

Harry: April, 1935 . . .

Kimiyo: The school used to be up there [nods in the direction of the Lodge At Ko'ele].

That's when the school was at Ko'ele?

I use to carry her and walk up [to the school, about a mile from their home near the fire station], and in 1938 the school moved down [rebuilt on the site of the present campus near Dole Park] next to the Japanese [Buddhist] Church—Christian now. My father said that over a thousand Japanese lived on Lāna'i for awhile. Then—during wartime, many were sent to Mainland.

I read about that in Harry's Brief History of Buddhism on Lanai, *published in* The Lanaian.

Kimiyo: I got investigated, too—from the FBI.

Because you had lived in Japan?

They asked me, "How did you learn English?" I said, "I'm not dumb. I go to night school, and Mrs. Carlson teach me English whenever she get time." I used to be dress maker, and they—the ladies in town—would come to my house and teach me English sometimes. That's how I learned English. [Laughs]. Then they said, "I know—I know—you're not dumb."

Harry: That's when they took in a few Japanese—Kishioshita, Hasegawa . . .

These were people sent to internment camp? [Harry nods]

What can you tell me about Dexter "Blue" Fraser? [The plantation manager following Bloomfield-Brown]

Kimiyo: Oh, he left 1956. He retired and moved to Kona [on the Big Island]. He was very nice man.

Harry, did you have any connection with Fraser when he was manager?

Harry: [Glancing at Kiyimo] Umm . . .

Kimiyo: Hardly, yeah?

Harry: No connection—although I worked in the beginning as a hospital orderly, and Fraser saw me and he thought I should be getting a different kind job. But that was only for a one month time.

Kimiyo: That's when Dr. Wilkinson was the only doctor.

That wasn't the same Dr. Bill Wilkinson who was here later, right? [Both nod]

Harry, when did you join the Lions Club? 1938. [Kimiyo produces a seasoned piece of fiberboard, lined with rows of attendance stars, that Harry had faithfully maintained the year he was the club's secretary.]

[*Author's note:* Harry died in January, 1997, followed by Kimiyo in July, 1999.]

The Matsumoto Family

Excerpt from *The Lanaiian*, February 22, 1952:

Miss Matsuko Kaya, gowned in traditional white satin, became the bride of Yukio Matsumoto on February 16 in an evening ceremony at the Lanai Buddhist Church. The Reverend Mineo

Miyasaki officiated and the bride's father gave his daughter in marriage.

She is the daughter of Mr. and Mrs. Teiichi Kaya and the bridegroom's parents are Mrs. Tai Matsumoto and the late Mr. Sajuemon Matsumoto.

The newlyweds will receive guests at the Block 21 Boarding House. They are both graduates from Lanai School and both are employees of Hawaiian Pine.

Excerpt from *The Lanaian*, July, 1962:

Yukio Matsumoto, Engineering Office Assistant, received a 20-year service pin in June, 1962. "Shoe" has worked at various jobs from field work during his school days at Lanai High, from being a painter, carpenter, light truck driver, electrical engineering clerk to engineering office assistant. His voice is familiar to all over KUA-250 [the plantation radio system]. He is also a whiz artist in his spare time, and loves to fish.

[*Author's note:* Yukio's nicknames—"Shoe," and sometimes "Shoemaker"—were bestowed by his school classmates in honor of his father's occupation as a cobbler.]

Excerpt from the *Honolulu Advertiser*, Sunday, March 5, 1995.

The first time the Lodge at Koʻele got into the *Conde Nast's Traveler* magazine survey, it went right to the top. . . . "We've been working harder," said Koʻele general manager Kurt Matsumoto. [*Traveler*'s "Readers Choice" survey for 1994 had placed Koʻele *first* among 50 tropical resorts.]

The following interview took place in the home of Yukio and Matsuko Matsumoto in their home on July 4, 1995:

Yukio: I was born on Maui in the year 1922, and my family moved to Lānaʻi in 1934 when I was twelve years old. That was with my parents—my mother and father, and my sister. We came over from Lahaina on the boat *Naia*. Prior to that, my father was unemployed because of bankruptcy, and he brought along the tools he needed to repair shoes.

He had been operating a shoe repair shop near Wailuku, and was doing fairly well. People that stayed at the [Wailuku] hotel who wanted their shoes repaired or shined would leave them at the hotel to be picked for repair during the evening, and by the next morning they would be ready.

Did he come here to do shoe repair work, or did he come to work on the plantation?

Because of his experience as a shoemaker, and since at that time there was not a shoemaker on Lāna'i, Mr. Okamoto and another person came to Maui to see him, and asked if he would move to Lāna'i. The location for his first shop was where the DIS-N-DAT shop is currently located [next to Richard's Shopping Center].

Where was he located later on?

The shoe repair business did not provide enough income to sustain our family, so the company told him that he could expand into selling second-hand furniture, so his shop was moved to where the barber shop used to be—where the Kaupe Cultural & Heritage Center is today [second building down from the Lāna'i Playhouse].

Where was the school located when your family moved over?

The school was located up by Ko'ele. The school buildings were not relocated [into Lāna'i City] until 1937. However, in 1938 I went to Japan with my parents for awhile where I learned cabinet making—so, I didn't get back and graduate from Lāna'i High School until I was twenty. However, because of my outside experiences, I bypassed field laboring jobs and ended up in the Engineering Department.

Where were you born, Matsuko?

I was born at Kapa'a on the island of Kaua'i in the year 1928, and my parents moved to Lāna‘i two days before my second birthday . . . and [smiles] I've been stuck on this island ever since.

Your parents worked for the plantation?

Yes, when we lived on Kaua‘i they worked on a sugar plantation. They thought that Lāna‘i was a better place with better pay, so my parents, along with my grandfather and my brother, moved here. I went to Lāna‘i School and graduated in 1946.

So, how did you meet Yukio?

I met him when I was working in the company storeroom as a stock clerk. He was with the electrical department at that time, and he would come in for parts.

When did you get married?

We were married on Lāna‘i at the Hongwanji on February 16, 1952, and we've lived in this same house from the beginning.

Yukio: But at that time it was only a two-bedroom house, and we had my mother and our son Colbert living with us. But about that time the company sold us the house, and I was able to get a second building—so, I knocked it down and used the materials to make this a three-bedroom house. Later on, we made it four bedrooms.

Matsuko, how about your career with the company?

I worked for five years, and after I had my first child I stayed home, but after my second child was born I signed up to work in the fields. I started as a pineapple picker first, and then they asked me to go as a temporary luna [harvesting gang supervisor]. Later I was promoted to field supervisor, and I finally decided to retire in 1987.

Yukio, who was the plantation manager when you came?

"Blue" Fraser was in charge when we arrived although Brown was officially the manager. However, as I recall, Brown was off on vacation and never came back—so, actually, Fraser was the man.

Bloomfield-Brown went away on vacation and never returned?

That's as I understood it at the time.

What do you think about what's happened to the island during the past several years?

It's changed . . . very much.

Author's note: Both of the Matsumoto's children left the island after graduation. One went on to law school, and practices in Honolulu, while the second majored in hotel management and returned to the island several years ago to become an executive with Lāna'i Company.

The Mitsunaga Family

News item from *The Lanaian,* December 17, 1948.

Effective December 1, 1948, Mr. Tamotsu Mitsunaga, formerly a Field Auditor, was appointed Plantation Budget Analyst with Hawaiian Pineapple Co., a newly established position on the Lanai Plantation. Mr. Mitsunaga has been with the company on Lanai since June, 1941.

"Tamo," as he is called by his many friends in this community, is married and has one child. His wife, the former Miss Sylvia F. Welch of New York State, is a teacher at the Lanai High School. He has been a resident of the community for 24 years and received his education at Lanai High. His parents, Mr. and Mrs. S. Mitsunaga are still connected with the Hawaiian Pineapple Company and reside here also.

Mr. Mitsunaga is active in sports and formerly played basketball for the Lanai High School in past years.

The following interview took place in the home of Tamo and Sylvia Mitsunaga on February 3, 1995.

Sylvia, how did you happen to come to Lāna'i?

I was teaching in a very small town on the Hudson River just north of New York City and was determined not to spend the rest of my life in a small town. [chuckles] When I graduated from college I told my best friend and classmate, Toni Lalla, that I'd give her one year, and then we were leaving for somewhere else. Actually, I had to give her two years—it was hard to pry her loose from her family. We discussed all kinds of places where we might go to teach—Saudi Arabia, Alaska, South America, Hawai'i . . .

Hawai'i made us the best salary offer, and I guess I primarily came for the money. Hawai'i paid so much more than what I was making in New York. During my first year here I earned a little over $2,200—with free housing. However, we had to pay three dollars a month into a fund to replace refrigerators and other appliances.

I was 23 years old in 1946 when Toni and I signed a two-year contract to teach at Lāna'i. As I said, I didn't want to live in a small town for the rest of my life.

We traveled from New York to San Francisco on a Greyhound Bus (that was all we could afford) and then sailed to Honolulu on the old *Mariposa* which had recently been released by the military so that the Territory of Hawai'i's Department of Public Instruction (DPI) could transport the several hundred teachers they had recruited from the mainland for the coming school year. The *Mariposa* had most recently been used to bring war brides from Australia.

Toni and I had been trying for months to find a way to get to the islands. At that time there were only two commercial flights a week from the West Coast to Honolulu. It was really a nice cruise. . . . It cost us $110 for the voyage—which included all of our food and amenities. It was just like sailing on a regular liner.

The school officials were really friendly and helpful. In fact, the Territorial Superintendent was on hand to meet our ship in Honolulu. Hundreds of teachers had been recruited that year to fill vacant positions throughout the islands' school system, so the man had, literally, a whole boat-load of adventurous young women to greet.

At that time there were no passenger flights connecting Honolulu and Lāna'i, except for Andrew's Flying Service which flew in every day to deliver the newspapers. So you had a choice: You could fly on the "paper plane," or go to Maui island and take the company boat.

We decided to take the paper plane.

There was no runway, as such—just a cleared place in a pineapple field. Actually, the location was the same site as where the present airport is situated, but there were no buildings—just a red dirt clearing. The plane landed, rolled to a stop, and the pilot tossed the papers out onto the bare red dirt—along with my bag—which broke open, spilling my things onto the red dirt.

There I was—being stared at by a group of field hands who had stopped working to watch the plane land—and, there they were, just leaning on their hoes, watching me gather up my personal and most intimate items.

I wanted to leave right then and there. I looked around. It was desolate—only pineapple plants for as far as we could see. "Where are the palm trees?" I asked Toni. "What is this place?"

If Principal Murray Heminger's wife, Agnes, hadn't driven down to meet us, I think I would have climbed back into the plane and left right then and there. However, Mrs. Heminger gave us a warm greeting, drove us into Lāna'i City, and delivered us to our assigned teacher's cottage.

We walked into the old wooden frame building and looked around, and I thought: *What is this place?* For the second time within an hour I was ready to leave the island.

The road from the "airport" into Lāna'i City [now known as Kamalapau Highway] was paved, as were the two main streets leading into town [now called Lāna'i and Fraser Avenues], and the streets running alongside the park [now, Seventh and Eighth Streets] were also paved—and that was it.

The street was not paved beyond the corner of Fraser and Seventh [present site of the Senior Citizen's Center] and on past the school, nor was the road running along the front of the teachers' cottages paved.

Most of the teacher housing you see today is fairly new—built in the early 1990s—except for two buildings still sitting on the corner as you drive into the housing complex. We lived in the second building. The one on the corner had been moved from the old school site at Koʻele. In addition at that time, there were several other cottages along the row—and during our first year more were built because there were so many of us crammed together.

The Hemingers lived in the "principal's house"—which was still located at Koʻele Ranch at that time [near the location of the Lodge at Koʻele's orchid house].

The faculty was much larger than it is today since school enrollment was close to nine hundred, and nineteen new teachers moved onto the island that year.

It was the practice back then for members of the Parents and Teachers Association to volunteer their efforts to clean the teachers' cottages before new faculty arrived. However, the best laid plans sometimes fall through the cracks, and our cottage had not had a face-lifting before we walked in. I remember it very clearly, because as I was scrubbing down the walls of my room the day after we arrived, the wall started moving away from me—the place was in really bad shape! However, some of the other units were worse than ours.

What did you know about the island before you arrived?

I knew I was moving to a place called Lānaʻi City, and I realized that it wasn't really a "city"—at least not like Buffalo, where I was born—or, New York City. With some searching, I had gleaned a small amount of information about Lānaʻi, and the DPI [Department of Public Instruction] had sent us a little bit more.

"Downtown" Lānaʻi City was about like it is now—not really

that much different. There was the park, and the stores around the park. The stores had different names then, but basically the town was about the same.

What was your first impression of the people and the town?

The people were wonderful. After we dropped our things off at the cottage that first day, Mr. Heminger came by and took us to the plantation office. It was late in the day, and we weren't sure what was going to happen—"What do we do now?" we wondered.

The first person to come through the door was Peter Piena from the company storeroom to tell me that my trunk had arrived and it would be delivered to our cottage in the morning. And then he told us that if we wanted to buy food we'd better hurry before the stores closed. [laughs] So we went to the store and picked up some basic items.

The following morning, Hector and Blanche Munro showed up at our door. I was taking Blanche's place at the school, as she was retiring, and Hector was a plantation superintendent. They would later play a very important role in my life, as Hector gave me away at my wedding.

The biggest impression I had of the town was that since most of the streets weren't paved, the cars had tire chains to provide traction when the streets were muddy. If you closed your eyes it sounded just like winter back home when cars had chains going clankety-clank on the snowy streets.

A concrete sidewalk connected our teacher's cottage with the school. However, it was usually covered with a layer of mud. So, we carried our shoes to school—walking barefoot—and when we got there we'd wash our feet and then put our shoes on.

What was the social life like?

It could only be described as "very busy." Every weekend something was going on. There was always a dance at what is now called "the old gym," and many parties at the Social Club [former plantation manager Bloomfield-Brown's home].

Members of the Social Club were Haole [Caucasian]—that

was a requirement—and included everyone living up on "The Hill"—commonly referred to as "Haole Hill," sometimes, "Snob Hill." Everyone assumed that since I was Haole, I was a member. However, I never paid my dues. It was just assumed that I belonged, although I never attended any of their activities. Actually the Social Club faded away around 1949, maybe 1950, as I remember. Social life was hectic.

How did you first meet Tamo?

There were a lot of young people on the island—many young single men working for the company—and there was a steady stream of boys showing up at the teacher cottages. On our first Sunday here, Tamo saw Toni at the Catholic church and he thought she was kind of nice, so he later showed up at our door on the pretext of selling tickets to the church bazaar. [chuckles] He was always very clever that way. He asked her out first, and a week after that we started dating. We got engaged in the fall of 1947 and were married in February of '48.

How did Tamo's family take all of this?

At first things were strained. I had met his sister because he had taken me to her house on New Year's Eve, and I knew his brother because he was in high school. But his parents and some of the other older Japanese people were trying to get him married to "other people."

One time we were on our way to a party and he said, "We have to stop at a house first." So we stopped, and he told me that I had to stay in the car while he went in. The reason for the visit was that inside was a group of older Japanese people that had "to talk" to him—very forcibly.

I had similar experiences when several of the people on "The Hill" basically told me, "You can't do this!"

At that time, Tamo was living in one of the bachelor houses in Lānaʻi City, while his family lived out at Miki Camp [near the airport], where he had grown up. Today, the old camp site is where the electrical generation plant is located [about a mile on the left going to the airport from Lāna'i City].

Eventually he took me out there to meet his family. I met his parents—his cousin—his auntie. And eventually, his auntie became our spokesperson.

After we were married, Tamo's mother treated me like I was one of her grandchildren—if she bought something for her grandchildren, she bought something for me. She would also drop by our home—often bringing along several of the older Japanese ladies. I always had to have fresh fish on hand because I never knew when I would be entertaining.

And what was the reaction of your family back on the mainland?

I only had several aunts. So, I called them up and said, "I'm getting married." And they said, "Fine."

So we got married at the Catholic church. Hector Munro gave me away, and we had a reception at what is now called the "Old Gym."

The whole town was there. Rows of long tables were set up the whole length of the floor. I don't remember how many people actually attended, but it appeared as if the whole town had turned out. It seemed that the buffet line never ended, and the containers holding the food had to be refilled three times.

So, where did you live?

We thought that was going to be a problem. I was living in teachers' quarters, and Tamo was in plantation bachelor quarters, and housing for young married couples in the village was in very short supply. But Tamo was working in the office, and when it was announced that one of the supervisory employees was leaving the island, he was asked if he would like the house. It was the only vacant one on the island. So, we moved into a hillside home where all of our neighbors were Caucasian. The rent was $55 a month.

Who was the plantation manager at that time?

Dexter "Blue" Fraser. He was very down to earth, with a fine sense of humor. For example, when they were paving the block in front of the school [actually, the street that now bears his name], he actually had a ribbon-cutting ceremony. I remember that it was on a Saturday morning, and I was just coming home from the grocery store, wearing shorts, a sweatshirt, and slippers—and he called to me, "Come, come on over, we're going to have a parade!" He had a real sense of humor.

What did you think of Manager William Aldrich, who replaced Frazer when he retired?

Oh, I loved the Aldriches. They were wonderful people. Her name was Billie, so they were called Bill and Billie. But I didn't really get to know them very well. I think I only went to their home just once—for cocktails. But he was quite thoughtful—good at doing little things. For example, when Tamo was presented a certificate for company service one time, Bill made sure that Tamo's father was there when it was presented.

How did things change at the school as the years went by?

The school population declined as people got older and passed through the child-bearing years. But, the old frame building classrooms were still very crowded. They were about half the size as they are now, and we had twice as many students as we have today. At one time I had 40 in my class. It was so crowded that I had to move my desk out because there wasn't room for it. There were two 100-watt bulbs in the high ceiling of the classroom, and in addition to being dark and gloomy, it was crowded. There wasn't a cafeteria, so we went to the kitchen to pick up lunch—rain or shine—and sometimes the swarms of pineapple bugs were really thick.

Tamo was responsible for the present school facility. Even before we had children, he was president of the PTA, and spent a whole year going back-and-forth to Maui. At that time the counties were responsible for the school's grounds and physical facilities, and they had promised Lāna'i a new school. However, the money went to Baldwin High School over on the island of Maui, instead. So, with the help of Pedro dela Cruz, who was in the Territorial House of Representatives, and Ruby Thalmann, another community leader and wife of a plantation supervisor, he went to the legislature for help.

What was the medical service like at that time?

At the time I came, Drs. Bill Wilkinson and Fred Reppun were the plantation physicians. Actually, the medical service was very good. We had the "old hospital," [a wooden frame building in the same location as the present hospital] and both of our children were born there. The main thing going on there seemed to be the delivering of babies—sometimes as many as five or six a week. To this day, Bill Wilkinson claims that all of those babies are still *his* babies.

How often did you go off island in those days?

As I said earlier, when we first came in 1946 there was no passenger air service, just the paper plane. However, Hawaiian Airlines did begin service that fall flying DC3s, but we didn't leave until Thanksgiving when we flew to Honolulu. After that, we maybe went to Honolulu every six months, or so. There was so much going on here that we didn't have time to go off.

So, how long did you teach?

In 1959, the year Hawai'i became a state, they built the school library, and I attended the University of Hawaii and started taking courses in library science. That was when I moved from classroom teacher to school librarian, the position I stayed in until I retired in 1982.

Do you have any outstanding memories of events during those years?

[Long pause] Yes. In the summer of 1947 the plantation experienced its first strike, which lasted three days. It was very scary. The atmosphere in the town was frightening. People said, "Don't go to the store!" We kept hearing all of these horror stories, so we just didn't go out. As it was summer, some of the teachers were working for the company, and they went to work. I didn't, as I was tutoring that summer. Unfortunately, the strikers mixed me up with one of the teachers that was working, and a couple of car-loads of union people came over and started yelling *my* name be-cause they had me confused for another teacher. They had found the right cottage—and they started throwing stones and garbage, and some of the teachers became very frightened and crawled out a back window and went for the police.

The next strike was just long—very long. It lasted nine months, but things didn't get violent. Tamo went to work so they could get out the payroll for the salaried people. I think the most memorable thing was the smell. The whole island smelled like one big rotten pineapple. When it was finally over, many of the teachers worked in the fields helping to bring the weeds under control.

Excerpts from a story from *The Lanaian*, January 6, 1956:

Others Who Served Gallantly in 1955

. . . there were others that gave their time and effort during the year 1955 toward the improvement of the community. . . .

TAMO MITSUNAGA worked as hard as ever in the role of Building Chairman of the local PTA when a snag was hit this year, and should be recognized for his community service. It should be said that Tamo and Mrs. Ruby Thalmann were primar-ily responsible for the acquisition of the new Lanai school.

With his skill in maneuvering government agencies into re-membering the Pine Isle, Tamo in his capacity as Vice Chairman of the Lanai District Boy Scouts of America, assisted by Chairman Elmo Tanner, was successful in getting a building for the Scouts from the county.

Prior positions he has held with respect to serving the com-munity were as follows: President of the Lanai City Lions Club, President of the Lanai PTA, Chairman of the Lions Club Sight Conservation Committee, Director of the LCWA, President of the HAPCO Federal Credit Union, and Treasurer of the Lions Club.

A View of Plantation Life in the 1960s

As stated earlier, this writer moved his family to Lānaʻi over thirty-five years ago to work for the plantation. The island was a great place to raise kids: horseback riding, fishing, an excellent swimming beach, hiking trails, hunting, and free golf. However, once the children graduated from high school there was little future for them on the island. The plantation didn't have the capacity to provide challenging jobs for young people, and since the island's teenagers had the opportunity to work in the pineapple fields during summer breaks from high school, they understood what "picking pines" was all about—and few wanted to make it their career. A few college boys returning for the summer had a chance at truck driving during the peak harvest season, and some were assigned to supervise work groups of visiting (off-island) high school students. Some of the girls returning for the summer were placed in clerical positions.

We'll never forget the day when our oldest son, Ralph, staggered through the kitchen door after completing his first eight hours working with a "gang" of his high school peers, trudging behind a harvesting machine, breaking off ripe pineapples, twisting off the crowns, and placing the fruit onto a conveyer belt which deposited them in a large bin carried on a flat-bed truck. As he kicked off his dusty field boots and pulled off the heavy canvas chaps (protection from the sharp tips of the plant's leaves), he glanced up and said, "Now I know why you have to go to college!" Up to that time he hadn't shown a real penchant for academics.

So, whether we liked it or not, it was understood that after graduation most of the young ones would leave . . . and we hoped they would go off to further their education and find success on the "outside." As I recall, only a couple of Ralph's classmates didn't go off to school or enter the military. We had a saying: "We export two things from Lāna'i—pineapples and kids."

In 1970 a select team of dreamers, planners, and managers put together the Lāna'i Development Plan, which was referred to as "a total conservation project," wherein agricultural lands were designated to be kept in agriculture (if not pineapple, then in cattle ranching, or other crops), conservation lands would be protected, continued forestation projects would protect the island's limited water resources, and two resorts would be developed to provide jobs and a future economic base for the island community. The plan included developing a select number of vacation-type upscale home sites for those looking for their Shangri-La on a secluded island only thirty minutes' flight time from Honolulu.

The Lāna'i Development Plan, however, never really got off the ground in the seventies, as neither internal nor external corporate funding was available. So, for several years, the Lāna'i Company planning team's dreams became nothing more than a collection of filing cabinets holding the unique, imaginative plans and programs.

SIX
Resorts—Par Excellence (1992–Present)

In 1985 the parent corporation experienced a major reorganization and change in leadership when Los Angeles businessman and entrepreneur, David H. Murdock, took over as President and Chairman of the Board. And that turned out to be exactly what the Lāna'i project needed, because Murdock not only had the wherewithal to get the finances of Castle and Cooke moving again, but recognized the unique character of the Lāna'i Island Plan, and its potential for a one-of-a-kind development. A few years later, plans to close the pineapple plantation were finally announced, but few Lāna'ians were adversely affected as most who were interested had already moved into the new resort positions.

Some critics of the change decried the end of the plantation era, primarily due to the loss of the plantation lifestyle. One Honolulu resident commented that he wanted to visit the island before it changed: "I've always heard about the humble way the people live, but I've never gotten around to going over there."

One Lāna'i community leader charged the critic with *zooism*. "It's the same as wanting to come here just to look at us . . . to see how the people live. Of course, he wouldn't live here himself. . . ."

Others criticized the plan on the basis that "the [plantation] workers have no practical hotel experience and can only be offered menial jobs in areas such as housekeeping, maintenance, or grounds keeping. . . ." One woman, a former plantation worker who had previously been offered only seasonal work in the har-

71

vesting department, but was now employed full-time in a hotel housekeeping unit, responded: "They have the nerve to tell me that I should spend the rest of my life on that damn plantation when I can work indoors all year around, away from the red dirt, mud, and rain—and earn tips."

In addition to constructing the two resorts, a diversified agriculture division was established, including a pork and poultry operation, as well as fruit and vegetable plots for production of organically grown produce for the community and the hotel's dining rooms. Cattle ranching was also reestablished (a reflection of days gone by) as well as resort recreation amenities, including horseback trail-riding, golf, tennis, and sporting clays.

All of the Hawaiian islands have nicknames. For example, the island of Hawai'i is called the "Big Island," the "Volcano Island," or sometimes the "Orchid Isle." For some seventy years, the island of Lāna'i was referred to as the " Pineapple Island." Now, it would be called the "Private Island," the "Exclusive Island"—or the "Elusive Island," as it had not only eluded Captain Cook's personal exploration of the mid-Pacific Ocean, but avoided any consequential economic development for the next century and a half. In retrospect, it had been a uniquely private island since the days when Walter Murray Gibson, and later Charles Gay, had consolidated the assorted land parcels under single ownership.

On January 9, 1990, the blessing of the Lodge at Ko'ele took place, and the ceremony for the Mānele Bay Hotel would soon follow. Each facility would be complemented by a championship golf course—"The Experience at Ko'ele," and "The Challenge at Mānele," and within a short time, both resorts would receive Five Star ratings.

The Mānele Bay Hotel is a handsome series of structures containing shops, dining rooms, a conference center, and 250 guest rooms. Its style is that of a Mediterranean villa, poised above the shoreline, looking out over the white sand beach of Hulopo'e

Bay—and on across to the Tomb of Puupehe perched on the sea stack above Sharks Cove.

The Hulopoʻe area has been designated as a State of Hawaiʻi underwater conservation district since the late 1970s, and the pristine cove is protected by a number of environmental use restrictions, including: no mooring of boats (except for native-style canoes), no throw net or spear fishing, and no removal of coral. However, shoreline pole fishing is allowed since the bay has historically been a favorite fishing place for the island's senior residents.

In addition to hosting small conferences and conventions, the Mānele Bay Hotel attracts visitors yearning for the classical Hawaiian vacation stereotype: a peaceful secluded place, gentle balmy trade winds, swaying groves of palms, and excellent snorkeling and underwater photography among a resident school of porpoises in the bay. The hotel's amenities include a pool and spa, a collection of personal health and grooming services, a distinguished art collection—and fine dining.

The contrasting Lodge at Koʻele, located on the site of the old Lānaʻi Company ranch (also the headquarters for the Lānaʻi Company in the 1970s when the island master plan was in process), attracts a different variety of wanderer. The architectural style reflects a 19th century English manor positioned in the midst of manicured rolling lawns, formal hillside gardens, fountains, waterfalls and rapids, a large reflecting pond, winding pathways, gazebos for private and peaceful reflection, an orchid house, flocks of wild turkeys strutting about the grounds, a fanciful eighteen-hole executive putting green, lawn bowling and croquet, and a heated pool to ward off the chill of the upcountry mornings.

The Lodge houses an eclectic collection of exotic paintings, sculptures, other art, and period furniture. Spacious verandas connect the three buildings that accommodate the 102 guest rooms, and feature massive wicker lounge chairs, decorated with a colorful assortment of Hawaiian quilted throw-pillows crafted by local artisans.

The hotel's focal point is the Great Hall. Massive stone fireplaces anchor each end of the two-story chamber, and an informal dining area borders the floor-to-ceiling windows looking out over the formal gardens. Between fall and spring, the afternoon fog often rolls down the pine-covered slopes of Lāna'i Hale, carried by trade winds drifting through the forests, and hotel guests congregate around the fireplaces for afternoon tea.

It is easy to imagine another time, perhaps a century ago, when it was common to hear that "the sun never sets on the British Empire," and imagine lounging in the great chamber of a titled, world-traveled Englishman—and enjoying his collection of art and artifacts acquired on trips around the world.

A series on Public Television, *Nature Perfected*, focuses on the development of European formal gardens and coined the series' title to describe their charm, grace and splendor—actually, an effort to enhance the natural beauty of nature's wilderness.

This rather describes what happened on Lāna'i through the years after George Munro (who later became a venerated Hawai'i environmentalist who retired on the slopes of Diamond Head) took over the Lāna'i Company ranch; and the Nature Perfected notion has certainly been accelerated during the past several years with the development and landscaping of the resorts.

The new visitor-based economy has had a significant impact on the island community, just as the coming of pineapple had six decades earlier:

For openers, there had been a shortage of family housing units for many years, since a majority of plantation employees had owned their homes since the 1950s, and as they retired their houses were not available for replacement workers. Also, with the plantation's final closing, many of the workers (being in their late fifties and early sixties) found it prudent to elect early retirement. The result of this was that the already existing housing crunch became exacerbated as people were recruited for the new resort-related jobs. Several hundred new housing units have been constructed for residents—and building continues.

As word went out to the island's residents that returning Lāna'ians would be given first chance at the new jobs, many who had left after high school returned to fill positions—most in management, professional, or technical areas where they already had experience or training. For example, a leading executive at Lāna'i Company is a third generation Lāna'ian who left after graduating from high school with no plans to return.

Many of the island's residents required training that could not be easily accomplished by the resorts' in-house programs, so the University of Hawai'i's Maui Community College was encouraged to establish a teaching center in the building that old-timer Nobu Kuwada identified as "Genevieve Oshiro's Fun House," and commenced offering classes, some taught by instructors flown in from Maui, as well as by interactive TV via the College's Sky Bridge System. Courses continue to be offered as residents (both former and new arrivals) require training for entry and/or upward movement in the hotel organizations, as well as in the community's other businesses, agencies and institutions.

In addition to the employment base provided by the hotels, the community supports the branch offices of the state's two major banks and a credit union, three general stores, a health food store, a service station, four restaurants, ten churches, a beauty salon, an insurance agency, gift shops and art galleries, medical and dental clinics, a community hospital—and several offices and buildings housing various federal, state, and county services, including postal, public health, senior recreation, police and fire. Today there are more than twice as many jobs on the island as there were during the plantation era's past several decades.

Prior to the advent of television reception in the fifties, the 1922-vintage movie house had served as a recreational focal point in the community, even though films shown on the island were sometimes a year old. However after TV became available, people lost interest, resulting in the movie theater's closure. But the newly arriving people, many with families who were used to modern cinema facilities, expected something comparable, so to make the island a socially competitive place to live and work, the old building was renovated, and the new Lāna'i Playhouse began featuring first-run films.

And other things changed. The public school's enrollment had dropped during the latter part of the plantation era as residents passed through the child-bearing years; but with the younger population arriving, student registration increased significantly, causing the need for additional facilities, curriculum, and personnel.

Art and culture also made their way to the island. Actually, many local artists had always been there but their talents only surfaced after San Francisco artist, John Wullbrandt, was selected by David Murdock to coordinate the hotels' Arts Program. The work of some thirty local artists, handpainters and quilters adorn the rooms and hallways at the Lodge at Ko'ele. The project was headquartered in a building adjacent to Maui Community College and remains today as the Lānai'i Art Center, a working home for many of the island's resident artisans.

The performing arts have also reached the island, as both resorts regularly feature lectures—including well known writers and travelers—as well as performances by popular and classical musicians. The events are free and open to Lāna'i residents, offering enrichment opportunities to those who live on a still somewhat isolated island.

SEVEN
What is the Crystal Ball Forecast for the Future?

This essay has pursued the history of the Island of Lāna'i from its volcanic creation, through the first settlement by native Hawaiians—and the ensuing environmental destruction by warring forces, the basic disinterest by the early European explorers, foreign activity during the early 1800s, and the later efforts at ranching and farming—ending after sixty years of successfully growing pineapple, until Third World production economics made the operation unprofitable—and finally the development of the new visitor industry program on the island.

Some observers question whether the island's entry into the tourism business will succeed, as some questioned Jim Dole's judgement in purchasing the island in 1922. They ask if financial success can come from operating two resorts with a mere total of 352 guest rooms. However, the comprehensive development program for the island goes beyond, as spelled out in the 1971 proposal to Maui County, to develop "programs for homes . . . including suburban residential. . . ." Ground breaking for future increments of development occurred several years ago, and upscale home sites (including fee simple town houses and single family units), mingle among the rolling fairways of the Experience at Ko'ele and the Challenge at Mānele golf courses.

Several years ago, an announcement was made that the diversified agricultural operations—but not cattle ranching—were closing down, and some wondered if the move was a prediction of more quandaries to come. But students of economic development in the Hawaiian Islands suggest that the combination of economies of scale, limited markets, transportation obstacles, and union labor (inherited at the closing of the plantation) were at cross-forces with the program.

Water is an issue—as it is throughout the State of Hawai'i. While sufficient water was developed to irrigate a large plantation and service a modern community, it was treated as a fundamental planning issue in the company's "total conservation plan" developed in the early 70s. For example: today's comprehensive water management plan calls for irrigating the golf courses with treated effluent.

On the development's positive side today, interestingly, is the island's relative isolation, and its thousands of acres of wilderness. As open space in Hawai'i continues to become a premium commodity, many individuals long for a rural lifestyle—but with the proper amenities of civilization: Open space, a Nature Perfected environment, cultural opportunities, surrounding wilderness, a safe community, and a thirty minute plane ride to Honolulu.

I recently boarded an IslandAir flight carrying a group of passengers from Honolulu to Lāna'i, and as we were settling in for the short trip I overheard the cabin attendant ask a lady passenger: "Have you been to Lāna'i before?"

"No, this is our first visit."

"You'll love it! My husband and I try to go over for weekends at the Lodge at Ko'ele whenever we can."

The Island of Lāna'i may, again, have found its appropriate place in time.

Further Recommended Reading

Over the years, a number of books have been written about the Island of Lānaʻi, and about the people who live here now, those who lived here in the recent past, and those fascinating people who dwelt here in the distant past.

These include such a treasure as Kenneth P. Emory's 1924 *The Island of Lanai—A Survey of Native Culture*. The late Dr. Emory was a distinguished Bishop Museum archaeologist who spent seven months studying the island at about the time the Hawaiian Pineapple Company acquired Lānaʻi. In 1974, he led a walk-around-the-island expedition with a dozen wannabe archaeologists and Hawaiian scholars (and they literally walked all the way—with Kenneth sometimes strolling barefoot through the sharp *kiawe* thorns). He had a keen memory, as well as being a tenacious old fellow. The following year Ruth Tabrah's *Lanai* was released.

A perennial favorite among locals is Robin Kaye's 1982 photographic essay, *Lanai Folks*, as well as Lawrence Gay's 1965 engaging small book, *True Tales of the Island of Lanai*.

In 1989, Arnold Savrann's photographic essay, *Lanaʻi, Hawaii* became available and is gracing coffee tables here and around the world.

These volumes about Lānaʻi are recommended to all who want to learn more about the island and its people. Some can be found in local stores as well as in hotel and airport gift shops, and most are available in Hawaiʻi's public libraries.

References

Ashford, Marguerite K. *Lanai: A Narrative History.* Paper prepared for the Department of History, Stanford University, 1974.

Castle, William R., Jr. *Hawaii Past and Present.* New York: Dodd, Mead and Company, 1914.

Degener, Otto. *William Hillenbrand, 1821–1886.* The Asa Gray Bulletin, Ann Arbor, MI, 1957.

Dole, Richard, and Porteous, Elizabeth Dole. *The Story of James Dole.* Aiea, HI.: Island Heritage Publishing, 1990.

Emory, Kenneth P. *The Island of Lanai: A Survey of Native Culture.* Honolulu, HI: B.P. Bishop Museum, Bulletin 12, 1924.

Hobdy, Robert. Interview, August 25, 1997.

Judd, Henry P. and Pukui, Mary Kawena. *Introduction To The Hawaiian Language.* Honolulu, HI: Tong Publishing Co, 1945.

Lydgate, John. "Reminiscences Of An Amateur Collector." *Hawaiian Annual, 1921.* Honolulu, HI: Thomas C. Thrum, 1920.

Munro, George C. "The Story of Lanai." (Undated manuscript believed to have been completed around 1955.)

Nellist, George F. ed. *The Story of Hawaii and Its Builders.* Territory of Hawaii: Honolulu *Star-Bulletin,* Ltd., 1925.

"Proposal To Revise The Maui County Interim General Plan For The Island Of Lanai." Lanai Co. file document 20. December, 1971.

Savrann, Arnold. *Lanai Hawaii.* Arnold Savrann/Castle & Cooke, Inc: 1989.

Stearns, Harold T. *Geology and Ground-Water Resources of the Islands of Lanai and Kahoolawe, Hawaii.* Honolulu, TH: U.S. Geographical Survey, 1940.

Tabrah, Ruth. *Lanai.* Norfolk Island, Australia: Island Heritage Limited, 1976.

Wentworth, C. *The Geology of Lanai*. Honolulu, HI: B.P. Bishop Museum, Bulletin 24, 1925.

Zschokke, Thedore C. *A Manual for Tree Planting in the Hawaiian Islands*. Honolulu, TH, 1930.